THE ULTIMATE IPL QUIZ

Berty Ashley is a molecular biologist with the Dystrophy Annihilation Research Trust and works with rare genetic disorders. What is not rare, though, is to see him conducting quizzes or attending them. Berty is also a lover of music, not only playing but collecting as well, as is evident by his growing stack of vinyl records from Jazz, Hindustani and Heavy Metal. He and his partner Akhila live in Bangalore surrounded by books, music and an assortment of pens and guitars.

Titash Banerjea is a co-founder of knowledge services start-up Gyaanspace and travel experience start-up Citybytes. He has been involved in designing and presenting innovative knowledge solutions whether it be live quizzes, online trivia games, or employee engagement and educational programs for schools. He is also a cricket fanatic and from childhood has taken great pleasure in hogging the television to watch every single match on television, whether it be Tests, ODIs, T20Is, IPL, BPL, CPL, Ranji trophy, KPL...as long as it's cricket, his eyes are glued. He loves sports, food and travelling and given a chance he would gladly do all three at the same time. He and his wife live in Bangalore and love attending pub quizzes and of course, winning them as well.

BERTY ASHLEY
TITASH BANERJEA

Published by
Rupa Publications India Pvt. Ltd 2019
7/16, Ansari Road, Daryaganj
New Delhi 110002

Sales centres:
Allahabad Bengaluru Chennai
Hyderabad Jaipur Kathmandu
Kolkata Mumbai

Copyright © Berty Ashley 2019

All rights reserved.

No part of this publication may be reproduced, stored in a retrieval system, or transmitted, in any form or by any means, electronic, mechanical, photocopying, recording or otherwise, without the prior permission of the publishers.

ISBN: 978-93-5333-409-3

First impression 2019

10 9 8 7 6 5 4 3 2 1

The moral right of the author has been asserted.

Printed at HT Media Ltd. Gr. Noida

This book is sold subject to the condition that it shall not, by way of trade or otherwise, be lent, resold, hired out, or otherwise circulated, without the publisher's prior consent, in any form of binding or cover other than that in which it is published.

CONTENTS

Introduction   *vii*

1. 2008: Blitzkrieg Begins   1
2. 2009: IPL's African Safari   6
3. 2010: Master Blaster Takes Charge   11
4. 2011: Whistle Podu Again   17
5. 2012: Korechi Lorechi Jitechi   23
6. 2013: Duniya Hila Diya... Finally   29
7. 2014: Circus Maximus Starts in the Desert   35
8. 2015: Rohit Lords over Eden   41
9. 2016: The Sun Rises   47
10. 2017: Third Time's a Charm   53
11. 2018: The Return of the Super Kings   59
12. Theatres of Dreams   65
13. IPL Potpourri   72
14. Record Makers and Match Breakers!   80

Epilogue   91
Acknowledgements   93

INTRODUCTION

On 25 June 1932 India played its first cricket Test match at Lords against England, becoming only the sixth team to be granted Test cricket status in history. 42 years later, on 13 July 1974 India played its first One Day International (ODI), against England once again, at Leeds. When Twenty20 (T20) cricket was introduced in 2003, just three years later, India played their first T20 against South Africa under the captaincy of Virender Sehwag and won the series.

On 13 September 2007, the Board of Control for Cricket in India (BCCI) announced that a new franchise-based T20 competition will be held in India called the Indian Premier League (IPL). With this announcement, cricket had found a new avenue, and India found a new fascination. In no time at all, the IPL has grown to become the most-watched and the most followed sporting event in India. The winners of the first season of IPL won ₹4.8 crore. The winners of the 2018 IPL won a whopping

₹20 crore. Since 2016, as per BARC, a company that collects India's viewership data, more than 300 million people have been watching the IPL series making it the most-watched cricket league in the world. In 2017, the IPL accounted for 0.6 per cent of India's Gross Domestic Product. As a brand, IPL is now worth more than $5,500 million. Only the National Basketball Association (NBA) and the English Premier League (EPL) have equatable figures. According to the BCCI's annual report, the IPL grew by 300 per cent in 2015-16—while Manchester United's (EPL's most profitable franchise) growth rate was 204 per cent for the same time frame.

India has a plethora of religions. If there are two things that bring together people of all faiths and beliefs, they are cricket and entertainment. What the IPL did was to cleverly bring both of these together. It is 'cricketainment'. The reach it has and the audience captivation it holds, allow it to have the kind of brand value that a company can leverage to launch their product—something akin to the Super Bowl in the US. It comes as no surprise that it has become the favourite launch pad for everything from electronic items to even movies.

An IPL season is now equivalent to a festive season in India, a festival that brings together people of not just different religions but states as well. No matter which team you support, you always enjoy the game and the performances of players from other teams as well. IPL offers incredible combinations which cricket fans could only dream about before, bringing together legendary sportsmen from across the globe for a common goal. Could you have imagined Virat Kohli, Chris Gayle and AB de Villiers, the top 3 batsmen in the world, in the same team? Could you imagine Sachin Tendulkar and Ricky Ponting opening an innings together?

The IPL has also become an excellent platform to discover hidden young talented players. It has opened up opportunities for a new generation of players, not limited by geography or economic status. Nitish Rana, Rahul Tripathi, Manish Pandey, Yuzvendra Chahal—these cricketers, through sheer hard work, perseverance and skill, have managed to climb the mountain of opportunity and make their presence felt on television screens across the world. Rinku Singh of KKR once contemplated working as a domestic worker to get his father a bike so he could do his LPG cylinder distribution easier. When he won a bike for being 'Man of the Series' in a tournament, he did just that. Mohammed Siraj, the son of an autorickshaw driver who taught himself how to bowl, played for Royal Challengers Bangalore in 2017 and went on to play for the national team as well. Thangarasu Natarajan, son of a daily wage worker and roadside seller from Salem, played for Kings XI Punjab and now supports his entire family. Kulwant Khejroliya, who spearheaded the bowling attack for RCB, used to be a waiter in Goa. Manzoor Dar, a former daily wage labourer and private security guard from Jammu and Kashmir, became a star batsman for Kings XI Punjab.

These are just a few stories showing how IPL has changed the life of cricket lovers.

Whether one likes it or not, IPL has changed the face of the gentleman's game forever. As we finish eleven amazing seasons of IPL and look forward to another decade of cricketainment, the authors present to you a selection of trivia and funda about the IPL seasons. Some questions will test your knowledge, some will test your memory and some will even test your logical reasoning! But we can assure you that you will remember amazing moments and re-live occasions that had made you smile, cry, laugh or yell at your favourite team—sometimes doing all that at the same time.

Happy Quizzing!

1

2008: BLITZKRIEG BEGINS

1. An Australian cricketer won the first of his two IPL Man of the Series awards in 2008. He later went on to score a century in an IPL final. Who was he?
2. In this edition, a Pakistani cricketer won the Purple Cap award. Who was he and which team did he bowl for?
3. Which was the only team in the IPL's inaugural season to have a non-Indian captain?
4. Who was the only English player involved in the first edition of the IPL in 2008?
5. Who was the first batsman to score a 50 and who was the first to score a 100 in the IPL?
6. Who hit the first four and who hit the first six in the IPL?
7. Who scored the first 150 in the IPL?

8. Who conceded the first four and the first six in the IPL?

9. Who bagged the first five-wicket haul in the IPL?

10. With 616 runs from 11 matches, which batsman had the highest number of runs in the first IPL?

11. With 68 fours from 14 matches, which batsman had the maximum number of fours in the tournament?

12. With 31 sixes from 14 matches which batsman had the maximum number of sixes in the tournament?

13. Who scored the fastest fifty in this edition, in just 21 balls when facing the Deccan Chargers?

14. Who scored the fastest century in this edition, in just 42 balls comprising of 10 sixes and 9 fours when facing the Mumbai Indians?

15. Against which team did Brendon McCullum of Kolkata Knight Riders score 158 from 73 balls and stayed not out?

16. Which batsman had the best batting average of 152 from 5 matches at the end of the tournament?

17. Which bowler bowled the most number of maiden overs during the tournament?

18. Which bowler had the best bowling average of 10.80 from 3 matches?

19. Which bowler had the best bowling economy of 4.80 from just two innings that he had bowled?

20. Against which team did LaxmiRatan Shukla of Kolkata

Knight Riders bowl just 5 balls and pick up 3 wickets and therefore, end up with the best strike rate of 1.66?

21. Which bowler conceded 59 runs in 4 overs against the Kolkata Knight Riders?

22. Three bowlers had a hat-trick each in the first IPL season. One was Amit Mishra from the Deccan Chargers. Who were the other two, belonging to the same team?

23. One of the most controversial incidents in the 2008 IPL was the 'slap gate' incident. Which two players were involved in the incident?

24. One of the first incidents of an umpire being suspended for taking a wrong decision was seen in the inaugural IPL. The umpire was Pratap Kumar. What was the reason for his suspension?

25. A dismal performance by one member of a team resulted in its CEO, who was a popular commentator, being sacked. Which team was it and who was the CEO?

ANSWERS

1. Shane Watson
2. Sohail Tanvir for Rajasthan Royals
3. Rajasthan Royals with Shane Warne
4. Dimitri Mascarenhas
5. Brendon McCullum
6. Brendon McCullum
7. Brendon McCullum
8. Zaheer Khan
9. Sohail Tanvir
10. Shaun Marsh from Kings XI Punjab
11. Gautam Gambhir from Delhi Daredevils
12. Sanath Jayasuriya from Mumbai Indians
13. Yusuf Pathan from Rajasthan Royals
14. Adam Gilchrist from Deccan Chargers
15. Royal Challengers Bangalore
16. Luke Pomersbach from Kings XI Punjab
17. Manpreet Gony of Chennai Super Kings
18. Shoaib Akhtar of Kolkata Knight Riders
19. Mohammed Hafeez of Kolkata Knight Riders
20. Deccan Chargers
21. R. P. Singh of Deccan Chargers

22. Makhaya Ntini and Lakshmipathy Balaji of Chennai Super Kings
23. Harbhajan Singh and Sreesanth
24. Referring to the third umpire without consulting his colleague
25. Royal Challengers Bangalore and Charu Sharma

2

2009: IPL'S AFRICAN SAFARI

1. Which two players from two different teams scored the maximum number of half centuries of 5 each?
2. Which player had the highest individual score of 114 against the Deccan Chargers?
3. How many sixes were hit in this season of the IPL?
4. Which wicketkeeper took the maximum number of catches (12)?
5. Which wicketkeeper had the maximum number of stumpings to his credit (8)?
6. Which fielder took the maximum number of catches (13)?
7. Which bowler took the maximum number of wickets?
8. Which batsman scored the maximum number of runs (572)?
9. Which team scored the lowest total in their opening

match of IPL 2009?

10. Which bowler took two hat-tricks in the series?

11. Which bowler had a remarkable inning of 5 wickets for 5 runs from 3.1 overs, in a match against Rajasthan Royals?

12. Which player scored the highest runs in an innings in IPL 2009?

13. Which player hit the most number of sixes in IPL 2009?

14. Which player from Kolkata Knight Riders conceded 58 runs in 4 overs thereby topping the table for 'most runs conceded in an innings'?

15. Which player from Chennai Super Kings topped the list for most runs scored from fours and sixes in an innings, with 10 and 5 respectively during a 98-run knock?

16. The highest match aggregate was 377 runs scored over 40 overs at a runrate of 9.42. Which were the two teams involved in this heavy-hitting match at The Centurion ground?

17. Which player was voted 'Man of the Series' and also had the highest combined run aggregate of season 1 and 2?

18. In the final match a memorable moment happened in the very first over, when the captain of one team bowled out the captain of the opposing team for a duck. Who was the bowler and who was the batsman?

19. What is the lowest total in this edition of the IPL?
20. Who was voted the 'Man of the Match' in the final for taking 4 wickets for 16 runs in his spell of four overs?
21. Which team won the Kingfisher Fair Play award in this edition of the IPL?
22. Which team finished at the bottom of the points table at the end of the tournament?
23. Which was the highest scoring partnership in IPL 2009?
24. Which team conceded the highest extra runs and against whom?
25. Who was the youngest player in IPL 2009?

ANSWERS

1. Matthew Hayden of Chennai Super Kings and Jean Paul Duminy of Mumbai Indians scored the maximum number of half centuries of five each in IPL 2009
2. Manish Pandey of Royal Challengers Bangalore
3. 29
4. Dinesh Karthik of Delhi Daredevils
5. Adam Gilchrist of Deccan Chargers
6. AB de Villiers of Delhi Daredevils
7. R.P. Singh of Deccan Chargers took 23 wickets in 15 matches
8. Matthew Hayden of Chennai Super Kings scored 572 runs in 12 matches
9. Rajasthan Royals scored the lowest total in their opening match against Royal Challengers Bangalore
10. Yuvraj Singh
11. Anil Kumble for Royal Challengers Bangalore
12. Manish Pandey of Royal Challengers Bangalore scored 114 runs which is the highest in IPL 2009
13. Adam Gilchrist of Deccan Chargers hit the maximum number of 29 sixes in IPL 2009
14. Mashrafe Mortaza
15. Suresh Raina
16. Chennai Super Kings and Kolkata Knight Riders

17. Adam Gilchrist
18. Anil Kumble and Adam Gilchrist
19. 58 runs was the lowest total ever in IPL at the time
20. Anil Kumble of Royal Challengers Bangalore
21. Kings XI Punjab
22. Kolkata Knight Riders
23. The highest partnership was between N. V. Ojha and Graeme Smith of Rajasthan Royals, for 135 runs against Kings XI Punjab
24. Chennai Super Kings conceded 26 extra runs in their match against Mumbai Indians
25. Kamran Khan was 18 when he took to the field

3

2010: MASTER BLASTER TAKES CHARGE

1. According to the designers, the gold foil lines on the front of the Mumbai Indians jersey for this edition of the IPL were supposed to represent an iconic landmark in their home city. What was the landmark?
2. How many balls did Yusuf Pathan take to score a hundred against Mumbai Indians in IPL 2010?
3. This South African seamer, known for his effective death bowling, starred in a Super Over on his IPL debut for Kings XI Punjab against Chennai Super Kings in 2010, within hours of landing in India. Who was this enthusiastic player?
4. Which batsman had the highest score of 127 runs in this IPL edition against the Rajasthan Royals?
5. Which batsman had the highest average of 59.00 by

scoring 236 runs over 7 matches?

6. Which batsman had the highest strike rate of 185.71, having scored 273 runs in 14 matches?

7. Which player scored the most number of fifties in this edition of the IPL (6)?

8. Which batsman hit the most number of fours (86)?

9. Which batsman hit the most number of sixes (27)?

10. Which bowler took the most number of wickets in this edition of the IPL with 21 wickets over 16 matches?

11. Which player had the best bowling figures of 4-4-13-1, with an economy of 3.25, in his match against the Deccan Chargers?

12. Which player had the overall best bowling economy of 4.06 over 3 innings?

13. Which team was at the bottom of the points table at the end of this edition of IPL having lost 10 of the 14 games they had played?

14. This edition of IPL became the first series to be broadcasted live on a video streaming website. Which website streamed the matches live?

15. Which batsman was awarded the Orange Cap for amassing 618 runs over 15 matches at a strike rate of 132.61?

16. Which player from Rajasthan Royals smashed 16 fours in his 83 run knock off 43 balls against Kings XI Punjab?

17. Who topped the table for 'Most Sixes in an Innings' with 11 sixes against Rajasthan Royals?

18. Which batsman from Mumbai Indians had the best batting strike rate of 185.71 from 14 innings?

19. Which bowler conceded 56 runs in 4 overs in a match against Rajasthan Royals and hence topped the list for 'Most Runs Conceded in an Innings'?

20. The very first tie of the 2010 IPL happened when both teams ended up with the score of 136. Which two teams were involved in this match that was decided by a one-over eliminator?

21. In an eliminator over, a Sri Lankan off-spinner was hoisted for a huge six by his National Team captain but in his very next ball, he took revenge by having him caught at long-on. Who were these two players who usually play on the same side?

22. This player was the costliest purchase at the 2010 auction, at a bid of $750,000. He then went on to make a mark with his all-round performance. Who is this Mumbai Indians player who took his team to victory over Royal Challengers Bangalore with a 13-ball 33 and a 3 wicket haul?

23. This south paw player was dropped twice in the final, once on 13 and then on 28. He went on to score 57 and thus helped his team to win their maiden title. Who was this player?

24. Which Indian player was declared the 'U-23 Success

of the Tournament' when he scored 419 runs from 15 innings?

25. In one of the last games of the tournament, two bombs went off while another was defused. As a consequence both semi-finals were moved out of this city. In which city did this security concern happen?

ANSWERS

1. Bandra-Worli Sealink
2. 37
3. Juan Theron
4. Murali Vijay of Chennai Super Kings
5. Kevin Pietersen of Rising Pune Supergiant
6. Kieron Pollard from Mumbai Indians
7. Jacques Kallis of Royal Challengers Bangalore
8. Sachin Tendulkar of Mumbai Indians
9. Robin Uthappa of Kolkata Knight Riders
10. Pragyan Ojha from Mumbai Indians
11. Doug Bollinger of the Chennai Super Kings
12. Virender Sehwag of Kings XI Punjab
13. Kings XI Punjab
14. YouTube
15. Sachin Tendulkar
16. Michael Lumb
17. Murali Vijay of Chennai Super Kings
18. Kieron Pollard
19. Albie Morkel of Chennai Super Kings
20. Kings XI Punjab Vs. Chennai Super Kings
21. Muttiah Muralitharan and Mahela Jayawardene
22. Kieron Pollard

23. Suresh Raina
24. Saurabh Tiwary of Mumbai Indians
25. Bangalore

4

2011: WHISTLE PODU AGAIN

1. In IPL 2011, Chris Gayle was picked up in the auction by RCB as an injury replacement for whom?
2. Which ground hosted the opening and the closing ceremonies of the 2011 Indian Premier League?
3. Which two teams made their first appearance in the Indian Premier League in 2011?
4. Whom did the Chennai Super Kings defeat in the final to win the 2011 Indian Premier League?
5. Who set a new record for most wickets taken in a single Indian Premier League season in 2011, by taking 28 wickets?
6. How many matches were played in the 2011 Indian Premier League?
7. A franchise from which Indian city played their home matches at the Jawaharlal Nehru Stadium during the

2011 Indian Premier League?

8. Who was the only player retained by Royal Challengers Bangalore going into the 2011 Indian Premier League auction?

9. Going into the 2011 Indian Premier League auction, the Rajasthan Royals retained two players; both were from the same country and had the same first name. Name the two players.

10. Which team made it to the top 4 of the league standings for the first time in the 2011 Indian Premier League?

11. Which side was bowled out by the Kolkata Knight Riders for just 81 runs in a match during the 2011 Indian Premier League?

12. In 2011, who became the first cricketer to become Man of the Match in an IPL final played on home ground?

13. Chris Gayle scored 608 runs in the 2011 Indian Premier League. However, he had played fewer matches than the second and third highest run scorers. How many matches did he play?

14. Among Indian bowlers, which seamer nicknamed the 'Ikhar Express' was the highest wicket taker in the 2011 Indian Premier League?

15. Who was the most expensive player in the 2011 Indian Premier League auction?

16. This player scored a century in a world cup final. He

would go on to become a coach of a winning IPL team. He was also the most expensive player for one of the new franchises in the IPL 2011. Who was this player?

17. Which former international captain came in as an 'injury replacement' for Ashish Nehra of the Pune Warriors India in the 2011 Indian Premier League?

18. Which Zimbabwe left-arm spinner who famously gave Sachin Tendulkar some trouble during Test matches, played a solitary match during the 2011 Indian Premier League against the Kolkata Knight Riders?

19. This cricketer made his IPL debut in 2009 for the Rajasthan Royals. He had a breakout year in the 2011 IPL season where he scored 463 runs for the Kings XI Punjab. Who is this player?

20. Chris Gayle scored 36 runs in an over in the 2011 Indian Premier League in a match against the Kochi Tuskers Kerala. The over included extras as well. Name the bowler at the receiving end.

21. Which captain hit the most sixes among Indians in the 2011 Indian Premier League?

22. Two batsmen who have hit two triple centuries in Test cricket, scored hundreds during the 2011 Indian Premier League. Name both of them.

23. Who was the leading wicket taker among spinners in the 2011 Indian Premier League? (He had dismissed Chris Gayle in the first over of the final match.)

24. Which Indian fast bowler had the best bowling figures

in an innings in the 2011 Indian Premier League taking 5 for 12 in a match at Kochi?

25. He was the Man of the Series in the 2010 Indian Premier League. However, he had to wait till 2011, to score his first and only IPL century. He achieved this landmark against the Kochi Tuskers Kerala. Identify him.

Answers

1. Dirk Nannes
2. M.A. Chidambaram Stadium, Chennai
3. Pune Warriors India and Kochi Tuskers Kerala
4. Royal Challengers Bangalore
5. Lasith Malinga
6. 74
7. Kochi
8. Virat Kohli
9. Shane Warne and Shane Watson
10. Kolkata Knight Riders
11. Rajasthan Royals
12. Murali Vijay
13. 12
14. Munaf Patel
15. Gautam Gambhir
16. Mahela Jayawardene
17. Sourav Ganguly
18. Ray Price
19. Paul Valthaty
20. Prasanth Parameswaran
21. M.S. Dhoni
22. Virender Sehwag and Chris Gayle

23. Ravichandran Ashwin
24. Ishant Sharma
25. Sachin Tendulkar

5

2012: KORECHI LORECHI JITECHI

1. This wicketkeeper from Haryana was the unlikely hero for Kolkata Knight Riders in the 2012 IPL final against Chennai Super Kings, scoring 89 in a high-scoring chase. Identify him.
2. How many teams participated in the 2012 Indian Premier League?
3. The top four teams of the 2012 Indian Premier League represented India in which other tournament?
4. Which franchise was terminated before the start of the 2012 Indian Premier League?
5. The ACA-VDCA Stadium hosted home matches for which team in the 2012 Indian Premier League?
6. Which international pop superstar, born as Katheryn Elizabeth Hudson, performed in the opening ceremony of the 2012 Indian Premier League?

7. Which side had 11 wins during the league phase of the 2012 Indian Premier League?

8. This cricketer once held the record for the fastest century in T20 internationals. He was adjudged as the Man of the Match in the first match of the 2012 Indian Premier League. Name him.

9. Which batsman hit left-arm seamer Sreenath Aravind for 6 consecutive fours in an over during this edition of the Indian Premier League?

10. Which bowler did Chris Gayle hit for 5 consecutive sixes in a single over during the 2012 Indian Premier League?

11. In a match between the Royal Challengers Bangalore and the Rajasthan Royals, AB de Villiers was presented with the Man of the Match award. He then proceeded to give it to a spinner from his team. Who was the spinner?

12. Driven by Lasith Malinga's haul of 4 for 16 which team did the Mumbai Indians bowl out for just 100 runs during the 2012 Indian Premier League?

13. In a 2012 Indian Premier League match between the Kolkata Knight Riders and the Chennai Super Kings at Chennai, Debabrata Das was given the Man of the Match award by his teammate, who had received it in the first place. Who was the original recipient of the award?

14. Azhar Mahmood, the only former Pakistan

international player to play in the 2012 Indian Premier League, represented which side in the tournament?

15. He would go on to captain a Hyderabad based team to victory in a later edition of the Indian Premier League. However, in the 2012 edition, he scored a brilliant 109 for his team while chasing in a match in Hyderabad. Name this batsman.

16. Which Rajasthan Royals bowler would become the subject of a controversy a year later, took the first hat-trick of this edition of the Indian Premier League?

17. A match between Royal Challengers Bangalore and another side was stopped for eight minutes at the Chinnaswamy Stadium in Bangalore during the 2012 Indian Premier League, as one of the light towers had stopped working. Ambati Rayudu was Man of the Match in this encounter. Identify the other team.

18. Who played a crucial innings of 40 runs off just 21 balls for the eventual champions, in the first Qualifier of the 2012 Indian Premier League?

19. Which New Zealand left-arm medium-fast bowler did Mahendra Singh Dhoni hit for the biggest six of the 2012 Indian Premier League (112 m)?

20. Which Indian opener hit a century in the 2nd Qualifier match, as the Chennai Super Kings beat the Delhi Daredevils to enter the IPL final in 2012?

21. This Australian cricketer led his team to victory in the 2002 Under-19 World Cup. Later in his career,

he was also named the captain of the Australian T20 international side. He had a fantastic 2012 IPL campaign, scoring 479 runs. Who was this cricketer?

22. In the 2012 Indian Premier League, which South African all-rounder smashed Virat Kohli for 28 runs in a single over in a match held at Chennai?

23. Which cricketer hit 59 sixes during the 2012 Indian Premier League (Just for the record, the next highest tally for the tournament was 20)?

24. Which batsman from the Delhi Daredevils played just 8 matches during the 2012 Indian Premier League, but scored 305 runs at an average of 61—which included a century?

25. Which Indian fast bowler was the highest wicket taker among Indians in the 2012 Indian Premier League?

Answers

1. Manvinder Bisla
2. 9
3. Champions League T20
4. Kochi Tuskers Kerala
5. Deccan Chargers (the stadium is in Visakhapatnam)
6. Katy Perry
7. Delhi Daredevils
8. Richard Levi
9. Ajinkya Rahane
10. Rahul Sharma
11. K. P. Appanna
12. Deccan Chargers
13. Gautam Gambhir
14. Kings XI Punjab
15. David Warner
16. Ajit Chandila
17. Mumbai Indians
18. Yusuf Pathan
19. James Franklin
20. Murali Vijay
21. Cameron White
22. Albie Morkel

23. Chris Gayle
24. Kevin Pietersen
25. Umesh Yadav

6

2013: DUNIYA HILA DIYA... FINALLY

1. In the 2013 Indian Premier League, all teams except one had Pepsi as their official beverage partner. Which team was it?
2. During the 2013 Indian Premier League, a spot fixing case was revealed which led to the arrest of three cricketers from which franchise?
3. During the 2013 Indian Premier League, the tournament had a new title sponsor, Pepsico. Whom did Pepsico replace to get the coveted spot?
4. Which team owned by the Sun TV Network made its Indian Premier League debut during the 2013 season?
5. During the 2013 Indian Premier League, the IPL governing council ruled that Sri Lankan cricketers would not participate in matches held in this city. Name the city.

6. Which famous rap artist from the USA performed in the opening ceremony of the 2013 Indian Premier League?

7. How many runs did Chris Gayle score in a match against the Pune Warriors India in this edition of the Indian Premier League, thereby setting a record for the highest ever IPL score?

8. Which left-arm seamer from Australia, who would also go on to receive a Man of the Match award in an ICC World Cup final, took two five-wicket hauls during the 2013 Indian Premier League?

9. The HPCA Stadium in Dharamshala hosted a few home games for which franchise during the 2013 Indian Premier League?

10. Which team topped the standings after the league phase of the 2013 Indian Premier League?

11. Which renowned fast bowler took 3 for 11 as the Sunrisers Hyderabad bowled out the Pune Warriors India for just 104 runs in their debut match in the 2013 Indian Premier League?

12. Rahul Dravid played his last IPL match in 2013. Which franchise did he play for?

13. Powered by a brilliant knock from Chris Gayle, which team made the highest total during the 2013 Indian Premier League?

14. Who became the youngest player to score an IPL half-century during the 2013 season?

15. Which side did the Sunrisers Hyderabad bowl out for just 80 runs in a match during the 2013 Indian Premier League?

16. Who emerged as the top scorer in the 2013 Indian Premier League season?

17. Apart from Rohit Sharma, which other Mumbai Indians batsman made more than 500 runs during the 2013 Indian Premier League?

18. Sachin Tendulkar played his last ever IPL match during the 2013 season. Name the ground where he played and the opponents he faced.

19. In a single match during the 2013 Indian Premier League, this batsman twice scored 28 runs in a single over. He also scored 26 runs in another over. Name the batsman.

20. Chris Gayle hit 51 sixes during the 2013 Indian Premier League season. Which fellow West Indies cricketer was second in the list of hitting the most sixes with 29?

21. Which Indian batsman scored six times 50 or more runs during the 2013 Indian Premier League—including a top score of 99?

22. Which South African batsman made a remarkable century after facing just 38 balls in a match during the 2013 Indian Premier League?

23. Who became the first bowler ever to take more than 30 wickets in a single edition of the Indian Premier League in 2013?

24. Who among the Indian bowlers was the highest wicket taker during the 2013 Indian Premier League?
25. Who was the only Indian to take a five-wicket haul during the 2013 Indian Premier League?

Answers

1. Mumbai Indians
2. Rajasthan Royals
3. DLF
4. Sunrisers Hyderabad
5. Chennai
6. Pitbull
7. 175
8. James Faulkner
9. Kings XI Punjab
10. Chennai Super Kings
11. Dale Steyn
12. Rajasthan Royals
13. Royal Challengers Bangalore
14. Sanju Samson
15. Delhi Daredevils
16. Michael Hussey
17. Dinesh Karthik
18. Wankhede Stadium, Sunrisers Hyderabad
19. Chris Gayle
20. Kieron Pollard
21. Virat Kohli
22. David Miller

23. Dwayne Bravo
24. Harbhajan Singh
25. Jaydev Unadkat

7
2014: CIRCUS MAXIMUS STARTS IN THE DESERT

1. Which stadium hosted the first match of the 2014 Indian Premier League?
2. Which former team India coach was signed as the coach of the Delhi Daredevils for the 2014 Indian Premier League season?
3. Apart from Abu Dhabi and Dubai, which other city in UAE hosted matches during the 2014 Indian Premier League?
4. Which team topped the league phase of the 2014 Indian Premier League?
5. During the 2014 Indian Premier League, who became the first cricketer to score a century in an IPL final?
6. Which Chennai Super Kings player made his 100th appearance during the 2014 Indian Premier League,

having played all his franchise's matches in the IPL till then?

7. Which team got bowled out for just 70 runs against the Rajasthan Royals in a match played at Abu Dhabi during the 2014 Indian Premier League?

8. In the 2014 Indian Premier League, a match between Rajasthan Royals and which other team ended with a Super Over, where the Royals won on the 'boundary count back' rule?

9. The 2014 IPL initially was held outside the country due to the Indian General Election. After 20 matches it returned to India on May 2, where the first match of this IPL was played between Chennai Super Kings and Kolkata Knight Riders. In which city did this match take place?

10. Which 42-year-old leg spinner took a hat-trick during the 2014 Indian Premier League?

11. Who was the only cricketer to make more than 600 runs in the 2014 Indian Premier League?

12. This West Indies batsman once held the record for the fastest century on his Test debut. He scored 566 runs during the 2014 Indian Premier League. Who was this batsman?

13. Which cricketer scored 552 runs at an astonishing strike rate of 187.75 in the 2014 Indian Premier League?

14. This Indian cricketer, known for his explosive batting,

has made two triple centuries in Test cricket. He rolled back the years during the 2014 Indian Premier League by hitting a century and scoring 455 runs. Who is this cricketer?

15. Who was the only overseas cricketer to score a century in the 2014 Indian Premier League?

16. A batsman from which side twice scored 95 in matches played in the UAE in the 2014 Indian Premier League?

17. Who was the top scorer for the winning side in the 2014 Indian Premier League final?

18. Which Dutch international featured in the final?

19. Which Australian international took a hat-trick, spread across two overs, during a 2014 Indian Premier League match against the Sunrisers Hyderabad?

20. Who was the Purple Cap winner in the 2014 season of the Indian Premier League?

21. In an innings of 68 off just 29 balls, which batsman hit as many as 9 sixes in a match against the Delhi Daredevils in the 2014 season of the Indian Premier League?

22. Suresh Raina made a remarkable 87 off just 25 balls in a Qualifier match held in which city during the 2014 Indian Premier League?

23. In contrast to previous seasons of the IPL, in which currency was the 2014 Indian Premier League auction held?

24. During the 2014 Indian Premier League, which leg spinner became the second bowler to take 100 wickets in the IPL?

25. During a successful run chase against the Sunrisers Hyderabad in the 2014 Indian Premier League, which cricketer scored a half century in just 15 balls?

Answers

1. Sheikh Zayed Cricket Stadium, Abu Dhabi
2. Gary Kirsten
3. Sharjah
4. Kings XI Punjab
5. Wriddhiman Saha
6. Suresh Raina
7. Royal Challengers Bangalore
8. Kolkata Knight Riders
9. Ranchi
10. Pravin Tambe
11. Robin Uthappa
12. Dwayne Smith
13. Glenn Maxwell
14. Virender Sehwag
15. Lendl Simmons
16. Kings XI Punjab (the batsman in question was Glenn Maxwell)
17. Manish Pandey (for Kolkata Knight Riders)
18. Ryan Ten Doeschate
19. Shane Watson
20. Mohit Sharma
21. Yuvraj Singh

22. Mumbai (this feat was achieved in a match against the Kings XI Punjab)
23. Rupees
24. Amit Mishra
25. Yusuf Pathan

8

2015: ROHIT LORDS OVER EDEN

1. Which team made a mammoth score of 235/1 in a match during the 2015 Indian Premier League?
2. Which left-hander finished as the top run scorer in the 2015 Indian Premier League?
3. This batsman from the Rajasthan Royals made a hundred each on his first tours of Australia, England and New Zealand. He made 540 runs in the 2015 Indian Premier League. Name this batsman.
4. Which West Indies batsman scored 540 runs for the Mumbai Indians in the 2015 Indian Premier League?
5. How many Indian batsmen scored hundreds during this season of the Indian Premier League?
6. Who made the highest individual score among Indians in this edition of the Indian Premier League?

7. Chris Gayle scored his only century of the 2015 Indian Premier League season against a side he would play for in the future. Name the team he made the century against.

8. Which Australian cricketer scored his first century during the 2015 Indian Premier League?

9. Brendon McCullum remained 100 not out off 56 balls during the 2015 Indian Premier League. Which side was he playing for?

10. Which batsman hit 38 sixes in this edition of the Indian Premier League?

11. The Purple Cap winner of the 2015 Indian Premier League represented which team at the international level?

12. Which Australian fast bowler picked up 20 wickets at an average of 14.55 during the 2015 Indian Premier League?

13. Which famous ground hosted the final match of the 2015 Indian Premier League?

14. The winner of the Man of the Series award in the 2015 Indian Premier League played for which team?

15. Which player was sold for a record ₹16 crore in the 2015 Indian Premier League auction?

16. The Sardar Patel Stadium hosted home matches for which team during the 2015 Indian Premier League?

17. Where would you find the Shaheed Veer Narayan

Singh International Cricket Stadium, which hosted matches for the Delhi Daredevils during the 2015 Indian Premier League?

18. Which famous stadium known for hosting football matches played host to the opening ceremony of the 2015 Indian Premier League?

19. Which team lost the second match of this edition of the Indian Premier League by just 1 run to Chennai Super Kings?

20. Hardik Pandya made his IPL debut against the Royal Challengers Bangalore in 2015. In the same match, one of his teammates also made his IPL debut. He was a left-arm seamer from New Zealand. Name the left-arm seamer.

21. Which city in eastern India, where no IPL team is based out of, played host to the second Qualifier match of the 2015 Indian Premier League?

22. Who was the top run scorer in the final of the 2015 Indian Premier League?

23. Rohit Sharma had a 131-run partnership with an all-rounder in the first match of this edition of IPL. Identify this all-rounder.

24. Courtesy a Man of the Match winning haul of 2 for 24 from this fast bowler, the Delhi Daredevils were bowled out for just 95 runs in a match during the 2015 Indian Premier League. Name the bowler.

25. Which Indian wicketkeeper batsman was bought for ₹10.5 crore in the 2015 Indian Premier League auction?

Answers

1. Royal Challengers Bangalore
2. David Warner
3. Ajinkya Rahane
4. Lendl Simmons
5. Zero
6. Rohit Sharma
7. Kings XI Punjab
8. Shane Watson
9. Chennai Super Kings
10. Chris Gayle
11. West Indies
12. Mitchell Starc
13. Eden Gardens
14. Kolkata Knight Riders
15. Yuvraj Singh
16. Rajasthan Royals
17. Raipur
18. Salt Lake Stadium
19. Delhi Daredevils
20. Mitchell McClenaghan
21. Ranchi
22. Lendl Simmons

23. Corey Anderson
24. Varun Aaron
25. Dinesh Karthik

9

2016: THE SUN RISES

1. The 2016 Indian Premier League final was held in Bangalore. It was originally supposed to be played in which city? (This city could not host the final due to a high court ruling which said that all matches scheduled after 30 April in the city were to be shifted to other cities due to severe drought.)

2. Which batsman scored a mind-boggling 973 runs in the 2016 Indian Premier League?

3. A batsman from Sunrisers Hyderabad scored 848 runs in the 2016 Indian Premier League. Who was this batsman?

4. Two left handers who had once played together for the Delhi Daredevils, scored 501 runs each in the 2016 Indian Premier League. One of them was the top scorer for India in the 2011 ICC World Cup final, and the other was India's top run scorer in the 2015 ICC

World Cup. Name both the players.

5. In this season of the Indian Premier League, the top four individual scores were all by batsmen from the same side. Which side was this?

6. How many centuries did Virat Kohli score during the 2016 Indian Premier League?

7. Which South African left-hander scored a brilliant 108 for the Delhi Daredevils against the Royal Challengers Bangalore in the 2016 Indian Premier League?

8. Steve Smith scored a century representing which side in the 2016 Indian Premier League?

9. Which Kolkata Knight Riders player scored 361 runs at an average of over 72 in the 2016 Indian Premier League?

10. Which Australian cricketer, nicknamed the 'Big Show', had an Indian Premier League to forget in 2016 when he scored 3 ducks?

11. Who hit as many as 12 sixes in an innings against the Gujarat Lions during the 2016 Indian Premier League?

12. Which all-rounder hit 8 sixes in an innings of 82, scored off just 32 balls during the 2016 Indian Premier League?

13. Which Bangladesh bowler took 17 wickets in the 2016 Indian Premier League?

14. He represented India in chess at the youth level. He took 21 wickets in the 2016 Indian Premier League for

the losing finalists in the tournament. Name him.

15. Who became the second bowler to take 6 wickets in an IPL innings, when he took a haul of 6 for 19 in a match against the Sunrisers during the 2016 Indian Premier League?

16. Which cricketer, known for his explosive batting, had remarkable figures of 4 for 8 to show in 4 overs in a 2016 Indian Premier League match against the Kolkata Knight Riders?

17. On which ground did Virat Kohli and AB de Villiers have a memorable partnership of 229 during the 2016 Indian Premier League?

18. Which franchise owned by Intex Technologies made its Indian Premier League debut in the 2016 season?

19. Which cricketer was the Man of the Match in the Gujarat Lions first three Indian Premier League matches in 2016?

20. Which team made it to the final of the 2016 Indian Premier League despite having to go through the eliminator stage?

21. In 2016 who became the first Australian to be awarded the Man of the Match award in an Indian Premier League final?

22. David Warner had an unbeaten 46 run partnership with an all-rounder to guide the Sunrisers Hyderabad to victory in the second qualifier match in the 2016 Indian Premier League. Who was his partner?

23. Moises Henriques, the Man of the Match in the Eliminator match of the 2016 Indian Premier League, was born in which European country?

24. Which former England cricket captain of South African origin played for the Rising Pune Supergiant in the 2016 Indian Premier League?

25. Which 45-year-old picked up 3 wickets conceding just 19 runs in the second match of the 2016 Indian Premier League?

Answers

1. Mumbai
2. Virat Kohli
3. David Warner
4. Gautam Gambhir and Shikhar Dhawan
5. Royal Challengers Bangalore
6. 4
7. Quinton de Kock
8. Rising Pune Supergiant
9. Yusuf Pathan
10. Glenn Maxwell
11. AB de Villiers
12. Chris Morris
13. Mustafizur Rahman
14. Yuzvendra Chahal
15. Adam Zampa
16. Dwayne Smith
17. Chinnaswamy Stadium
18. Gujarat Lions
19. Aaron Finch
20. Sunrisers Hyderabad
21. Ben Cutting
22. Bipul Sharma

23. Portugal
24. Kevin Pietersen
25. Brad Hogg

10

2017: THIRD TIME'S A CHARM

1. In the 2017 Indian Premier League, this cricketer scored a valuable 47 in the final. He made his international T20 debut for India in 2018. His younger brother also plays international cricket. Who is this player who once donated a blank cheque for the treatment of an ex-cricketer?

2. Which team ended up on the top spot after the league phase of the 2017 Indian Premier League?

3. How many batsmen scored more than 500 runs in the 2017 Indian Premier League?

4. This South African batsman is, at times, considered unsuitable for the T20 format. However, in the 2017 Indian Premier League, he dumbfounded all critics with 2 centuries. Who is he?

5. This English all-rounder scored his first century in the 2017 Indian Premier League. His team made

it to the Indian Premier League finals, although he was not able to take part in the match owing to his international commitments. Name him.

6. Two cricketers from the same team hit 26 sixes in the 2017 Indian Premier League. One was a right hander and the other, a left hander. The right hander, however, failed to make a single half century in the tournament. Name both the cricketers in question.

7. He is a two time Indian Premier League winning captain. He scored 498 runs in the 2017 Indian Premier League with four half centuries. He has also been the highest scorer for his country in an ICC World T20 final. Who is he?

8. This bowler was the highest wicket taker among left-armers in the 2017 Indian Premier League. He was also the highest paid Indian in the 2018 Indian Premier League auction. Can you guess who he is?

9. Which Indian fast bowler, who played a starring role in India's first ever Test series win against Australia, took 20 wickets in the 2017 Indian Premier League?

10. Which international captain was the top scorer among right handers in the 2017 Indian Premier League?

11. Which cricketer from Karnataka scored five half centuries in the 2017 Indian Premier League?

12. Among spin bowlers, who was the highest wicket taker in the 2017 Indian Premier League?

13. Which two bowlers took hat-tricks on the same day in

the 2017 Indian Premier League?

14. Which West Indian made a half century in just 15 balls during the 2017 Indian Premier League?

15. During his innings of 97 off just 43 balls against Gujarat Lions in the 2017 Indian Premier League, which young Indian left hander hit 9 sixes?

16. Which team won an eliminator match during this season of the 2017 Indian Premier League, despite batting for only 5.2 overs?

17. Which city hosted the final of the 2017 Indian Premier League?

18. Which businessman was the owner of the team that made it to the final of the 2017 Indian Premier League, but did not feature in the 2018 edition?

19. This team made it to the final of the 2016 Indian Premier League, but ended up at the bottom of the standings after the league phase of the 2017 Indian Premier League. Which team was it?

20. This cricketer was born on 5 October at 5:05 AM and hence decided to wear jersey No. 555. Who was this player who featured in the final of the 2017 Indian Premier League?

21. Which team beat the Delhi Daredevils by a margin of 146 runs in a match during the 2017 Indian Premier League?

22. This cricketer was the subject of controversy for wearing jersey No. 10 for India in an international

match. He had an IPL to forget with the bat, going out for a duck in all 3 innings that he batted in IPL 2017. Who was he?

23. This batsman, who played for Delhi Daredevils in the 2017 Indian Premier League, has represented India in one T20 international match. He scored 102 against the Rising Pune Supergiant during the 2017 Indian Premier League. Name him.

24. This Australian batsman scored 295 runs in just 7 matches at a strike rate of more than 180 during the 2017 Indian Premier League season. Name him.

25. Which two time Purple Cap winner took a brilliant haul of 5 for 19 against the Kings XI Punjab in the 2017 Indian Premier League?

Answers

1. Krunal Pandya
2. Mumbai Indians
3. 1 (David Warner made 641 runs)
4. Hashim Amla
5. Ben Stokes
6. Glen Maxwell and David Warner
7. Gautam Gambhir
8. Jaydev Unadkat
9. Jasprit Bumrah
10. Steve Smith
11. Robin Uthappa
12. Imran Tahir
13. Andrew Tye and Samuel Badree
14. Sunil Narine
15. Rishabh Pant
16. Kolkata Knight Riders
17. Hyderabad
18. Sanjiv Goenka
19. Royal Challengers Bangalore
20. Washington Sundar
21. Mumbai Indians
22. Shardul Thakur

23. Sanju Samson
24. Chris Lynn
25. Bhuvneshwar Kumar

11

2018: THE RETURN OF THE SUPER KINGS

1. Name the only cricketer from Kashmir to play in 2018 Indian Premier League?
2. Who is the highest paid Under-19 player in 2018 Indian Premier League?
3. Jhanvi Mehta, who was sitting at the 2018 IPL auction, is the daughter of which Bollywood actress?
4. Who won the Perfect Catch Award in 2018 Indian Premier League?
5. Who hit the most number of sixes in 2018 Indian Premier League?
6. In the 2018 Indian Premier League, which international captain emerged as the leading run scorer of the tournament?
7. This left hander scored 684 runs in the 2018 Indian

Premier League, with 37 sixes to his credit. Identify him.

8. Who was the highest scorer of the series for the winning team in the 2018 Indian Premier League?

9. This Australian cricketer made 555 runs in the 2018 Indian Premier League. He also became the first overseas cricketer to score a century in an Indian Premier League final. Name him.

10. Which English cricketer made more than 500 runs in the 2018 Indian Premier League with five half centuries?

11. This captain of an international team scored 530 runs in this edition of the Indian Premier League. He scored over 50 four times. Unfortunately, his side ended up in sixth spot on the league table. Identify him.

12. This franchise had as many as six different players scoring more than 300 runs in the 2018 Indian Premier League. Which franchise is this?

13. Apart from Rishabh Pant, who was the only left hander to score a century in the 2018 Indian Premier League?

14. Among all the cricketers to score more than 400 runs in the 2018 season of the Indian Premier League, who had the highest batting average?

15. In the 2018 Indian Premier League a side lost to another side as many as four times. Name the two sides in question.

16. Among Indian bowlers, who was the highest wicket taker in the 2018 Indian Premier League?

17. The top wicket taker of the 2018 Indian Premier League played international cricket for which country?

18. This Indian cricketer has been the subject of controversy recently. He had a very good 2018 Indian Premier League with the ball, taking 18 wickets at an average of 21.16. Name him.

19. This young fast bowler was the subject of several memes when he was picked up by Chennai Super Kings at the 2018 IPL auction. He took a brilliant haul of 4 for 10 against Kings XI Punjab in the same season. Who was he?

20. Bowlers from a single franchise took 4 wickets or more in an innings in the 2018 Indian Premier League four times. Name the franchise.

21. This young leg spinner plays for Punjab in the Ranji Trophy. He represented Mumbai Indians in the 2018 Indian Premier League and took a haul of 3 for 23 on his debut. Name him.

22. Which side played its home matches at the Maharashtra Cricket Association (MCA) stadium in the 2018 Indian Premier League?

23. Two cricketers from the same international team hit 11 sixes individually in an innings in a 2018 Indian Premier League match. Name both the players.

24. This batsman played for a team which has recently

changed its name. He scored 28 runs in an over against the Kolkata Knight Riders in the 2018 Indian Premier League, including 4 sixes. Name this player.

25. A cricketer from which nation hit as many as eight half centuries in the 2018 Indian Premier League?

Answers

1. Manzoor Dar
2. Mujeeb Zadran of Afghanistan
3. Juhi Chawla
4. Trent Boult
5. Rishabh Pant
6. Kane Williamson
7. Rishabh Pant
8. Ambati Rayudu
9. Shane Watson
10. Jos Buttler
11. Virat Kohli
12. Kolkata Knight Riders
13. Chris Gayle
14. M.S. Dhoni
15. Sunrisers Hyderabad and Chennai Super Kings
16. Siddharth Kaul
17. Australia
18. Hardik Pandya
19. Lungi Ngidi
20. Kings XI Punjab
21. Mayank Markande
22. Chennai Super Kings

23. Andre Russell and Chris Gayle
24. Shreyas Iyer
25. New Zealand (cricketer in question was Kane Williamson)

12
THEATRES OF DREAMS

1. Which venue in India has hosted the maximum number of matches (74)?
2. Which overseas venue has hosted the most number of matches (15)?
3. Which has been the home stadium of Kings XI Punjab from 2008-2018?
4. Which team has been based out of the Eden Gardens, since 2008?
5. For which team has the Sawai Mansingh Stadium in Jaipur been home since 2008?
6. The Dr Y.S. Rajashekhar Reddy ACA-VDCA Cricket Stadium is one of the most well maintained stadiums, where grass for the outfield was specially imported from the Caribbean. In which city is it found?
7. In 2011, Kochi Tuskers Kerala and Kings XI Punjab

both had the Holkar Stadium as their home stadium. Named after the dynasty that ruled the region, where is this stadium situated?

8. Between 2010 and 2013, Kings XI Punjab were based out of the HPCA stadium. This picturesque venue is situated at an altitude of 1,457 m above the sea level and has the snow-capped Himalayan Mountains in the background. In which city is this stadium located and what does the HPCA stand for?

9. The Vidarbha Cricket Association Stadium is the largest cricket stadium in India in terms of field area and was the home base for the Deccan Chargers in 2010. In which city is it situated?

10. The Sardar Patel Stadium, also known as the 'Motera' Stadium, was the home base for the Rajasthan Royals from 2010 to 2015. It is currently under renovation and when re-opened, it will be the largest cricket stadium in the world with a seating capacity of 110,000 spectators, overtaking the Melbourne Cricket Ground in Australia. In which city is this situated?

11. The Barabati Stadium was established in 1958. It has been the home base for various teams over the years such as Deccan Chargers, Kings XI Punjab and Kolkata Knight Riders. In which city is it situated?

12. This stadium in Mumbai was established in 1937. It is named after the then governor of Bombay (now Mumbai) who was asked by the secretary of the

BCCI—'Your excellency, which would you prefer to accept from sportsmen, money for your government, or immortality for yourself?' He chose immortality and gave 90,000 square yards of land to build a stadium. What is the name of this stadium?

13. The Green Park Stadium is built near the river Ganges and is named after a British lady, Madam Green, who used to go there for horse riding. The stadium is nicknamed 'Billiards Table'. It was the home base of the Gujarat Lions in 2016-2017. In which city is this situated?

14. The Newlands Cricket Ground is regarded as one of the most beautiful cricket grounds in the world, being overlooked by the Table Mountain and the Devil's Peak. It has hosted 7 matches of the 2009 IPL series. In which city is this situated?

15. The Kingsmead Cricket Ground in Durban hosted 15 matches of the 2009 IPL series. There, a famous myth does the rounds that a certain natural phenomenon affects the batting conditions as the stadium is built quite close to the beach. What phenomenon is supposed to affect the batting in this stadium?

16. The St George's Park Cricket Ground is one of the oldest venues in the world, having hosted its first match in 1889. The ground is notable for its brass band that plays during major matches, adding a unique flavour to its atmosphere. It hosted seven matches during the 2009 IPL season. In which

picturesque city is it situated?

17. This stadium in Johannesburg, which hosted eight matches during the 2009 season, is nicknamed 'The Bullring' due to its design and intimidating atmosphere. By which name do we know it? Its name sounds more like an 80's pop band's.

18. This stadium in Kimberley hosted three matches during the 2009 IPL season. It is known as the 'Diamond Oval' and has been associated with, and named after, a certain company that is the world's largest producer of diamonds. Which company is this?

19. The Sheikh Zayed Stadium in Abu Dhabi was opened in 2004. Along with two other stadiums, it hosted multiples matches in a particular season. Which season was this and what was the reason for that season shifting out of India?

20. The Sharjah Cricket Stadium was established in 1982 and has hosted six IPL matches. At the behest of local cricketing patron Abdul Rahman Bukhatir, the Sharjah Cricket Stadium became the home ground of which international team in 2010?

21. The Dubai International Cricket Stadium hosted seven IPL matches after its establishment in 2009. It is lit by a special system of 350 floodlights that are fixed around the circumference of its round roof, thereby minimizing the shadows of objects in the ground and having no light towers. What name is given to this

lighting system that sounds like something from a J.R.R. Tolkien novel?

22. As part of a 'Go Green' initiative, this stadium became the first in the world to use solar panels to generate bulk of the electricity needed to run the stadium. Named after the BCCI president from 1977-1980, which stadium is this?

23. This stadium has been the home base of the Delhi Daredevils since 2008. It is named after the Sultan of Delhi, who ruled from 1351 to 1388. What is the name of this stadium, which has seen multiple records being established?

24. This stadium was designed in 1861. An urban legend says that the then zamindar, Babu Rajchandra Das, gifted one of his biggest gardens besides river Hooghly to Viceroy Lord Auckland and his sister Emily after they had saved one of his daughters from a fatal disease. Subsequently from then onwards the name was changed from Mar Bagan to its present name. How do we know the ground today?

25. This iconic stadium was established in 1916 and it has been the epicentre of various historic moments in cricket. The home of the Chennai Super Kings since 2008 it is named after the former president of the BCCI. What is the name of this stadium?

ANSWERS

1. M. Chinnaswamy Stadium in Bangalore
2. Kingsmead Cricket Ground in Durban
3. PCA Stadium, Mohali
4. Kolkata Knight Riders
5. Rajasthan Royals
6. Vishakapatttanam
7. Indore
8. Dharmashala, Himachal Pradesh Cricket Association
9. Nagpur in Maharashtra
10. Ahmedabad in Gujarat
11. Cuttack in Odisha
12. Brabourne Stadium
13. Kanpur
14. Cape Town, South Africa
15. The rise and fall of the tide
16. Port Elizabeth
17. The Wanderers
18. De Beers
19. In 2014, due to the General Elections in India
20. Afghanistan Cricket Team
21. Ring of Fire
22. M. Chinnaswamy Stadium in Bangalore

23. Feroz Shah Kotla Ground, Delhi
24. Eden Gardens
25. Muttaiya Annamalai Chidambaram Stadium, Chennai

13
IPL POTPOURRI

1. How many finals has Mahendra Singh Dhoni played in the IPL?
2. Which cricketer has scored the fastest hundred in the IPL?
3. Which team has successfully defended its title in the IPL?
4. How many foreign (overseas) captains have won the IPL?
5. Which cricketer has bowled the most number of dot balls in the IPL?
6. How many hat-tricks have taken place in the IPL?
7. Which teams have collectively won the most number of Indian Premier League titles since 2008?
8. In which of the IPL editions, the record for most sixes was set with 872 sixes hit across 51 matches?

9. At the end of the 2018 edition, which player had scored the highest numbers of runs in IPL history?
10. Which player has taken the most number of wickets in IPL so far?
11. Who has hit the most number of sixes in the history of the IPL?
12. Which team has won the highest numbers of IPL matches across all the seasons?
13. Which bowler has taken the most number of hat-tricks across the IPL seasons?
14. Who has taken the most catches in the history of the IPL?
15. Who has been the costliest player in IPL auction history?
16. Which cricketer has been awarded the maximum number of IPL titles?
17. Who is the only overseas bowler to have topped the wicket charts in two IPL seasons?
18. Which fast bowler took a hat-trick on his IPL debut?
19. Which player has conceded the most number of sixes in the IPL?
20. Who is the only player to be named Man of the Match in an IPL final while playing for the losing side?
21. Which cricketer has the most ducks to his credit in the IPL?
22. What is the highest score scored in an IPL match?

23. Who is the oldest player to have played in the IPL?
24. Why is cricketer Lakshmipathy Balaji (CSK) so significant in the IPL record books?
25. Which team has won the most number of IPL Fair Play Awards?
26. Which Australian player has played for seven different IPL teams?
27. Who has scored the fastest 50 in IPL history?
28. Whose record for the fastest hundred did Chris Gayle break when he scored the fastest IPL hundred of all time against the Pune Warriors India?
29. Who has bowled the most number of maiden overs in IPL history?
30. Who has scored the most number of sixes in an IPL innings?
31. Who has scored the most number of hundreds in the history of the IPL?
32. Who has bowled the most number of dot balls in IPL history?
33. Who has the best bowling figures in the history of the IPL?
34. Among all the bowlers who have played more than 50 IPL matches, who has the all-time best bowling economy rate?
35. At the end of the 2018 season, which player had scored the most number of fours in IPL history?

36. Which team has recorded the lowest total in IPL history?

37. Which team has recorded the highest total in IPL history?

38. This highly disciplined leg-spinner had bowled an astonishing 386 overs without bowling a no-ball over the course of 8 years. Who was this bowler who finally bowled a no-ball against the Delhi Daredevils in 2016?

39. In the very first IPL match in 2008, when Brendon McCullum struck 158 off 73 balls for KKR against Royal Challengers, who became the first Pakistan player to play in the IPL?

40. Among all cricketers to score more than 4,000 runs in the Indian Premier League, who has the best batting average?

41. How many players have hit more than 200 sixes in the Indian Premier League?

42. Playing for the Deccan Chargers, who became the first left hander to hit 10 or more sixes in an IPL innings?

43. Who holds the record for the highest individual score by an Indian in IPL history?

44. The highest strike rate ever recorded in an IPL innings of more than 30 runs was by an all-rounder playing for the Delhi Daredevils franchise against the Rising Pune Supergiant. Name the all-rounder.

45. This cricketer has scored 36 half centuries in the IPL without completing a hundred. He has also played a

starring role for his country in the finals of two ICC tournaments. Name him.

46. Among Indian cricketers, who has scored the highest number of IPL centuries?

47. Among non-Asian cricketers who has taken the maximum number of IPL wickets?

48. Among uncapped Indian bowlers, this fast bowler recorded the best ever IPL figures, taking 5 for 14 in a 2018 match. Who is he?

49. Apart from Amit Mishra, who is the only bowler to take multiple IPL hat-tricks?

50. Who holds the record for the best bowling figures by a Kings XI Punjab bowler in an IPL final, taking 4 wickets against the Kolkata Knight Riders?

Answers

1. Seven
2. Chris Gayle
3. Chennai Super Kings
4. Three
5. Praveen Kumar
6. Seventeen
7. Chennai Super Kings and Mumbai Indians
8. IPL 2018
9. Suresh Raina
10. Lasith Malinga
11. Chris Gayle
12. Mumbai Indians
13. Amit Mishra (3 hat-tricks)
14. Suresh Raina
15. Yuvraj Singh
16. Rohit Sharma
17. Dwayne Bravo took 32 wickets for Chennai Super Kings in 2013. He also led the way in 2015 with 24 wickets.
18. Andrew Tye. For Gujarat Lions against Rising Pune Supergiant
19. Amit Mishra has been hit for 150 sixes
20. Anil Kumble in the 2009 final

21. Harbhajan Singh
22. 263
23. Brad Hogg
24. He was the first player to take a hat-trick in IPL
25. Chennai Super Kings
26. Aaron Finch
27. Lokesh Rahul smashed the fastest fifty off just 14 balls
28. Yusuf Pathan
29. Praveen Kumar
30. Chris Gayle has hit 17 sixes in the match against Pune Warriors
31. Chris Gayle has scored 6 hundreds in IPL
32. Harbhajan Singh has bowled 1,128 dot balls in IPL so far
33. Sohail Tanvir's 6 for 14 is the best bowling figure in the IPL
34. Sunil Narine has the all-time best bowling economy of 6.53
35. Gautam Gambhir has hit 491 fours in IPL
36. Royal Challengers Bangalore were wiped out for just 49 runs against Kolkata Knight Riders
37. Royal Challengers Bangalore scored a gigantic total of 263/5 against Pune Warriors India
38. Piyush Chawla
39. Mohammad Hafeez

40. David Warner (4,014 runs at 40.54)
41. 1 (Chris Gayle with 292)
42. Adam Gilchrist
43. Rishabh Pant (128*)
44. Chris Morris
45. Gautam Gambhir
46. Virat Kohli
47. Dwayne Bravo
48. Ankit Rajpoot
49. Yuvraj Singh
50. Karanveer Singh (However, he ended up on the losing side and also conceded 54 runs in the process.)

14

RECORD MAKERS AND MATCH BREAKERS!

1. A maximum of how many foreign players can play in the playing eleven of a team in an IPL match?
2. Which world cup winning captain was signed by the Pune Warriors India, who lost every single of the 6 matches that he played?
3. The very first IPL match was played between Royal Challengers Bangalore and the Kolkata Knight Riders. The 500th game of the IPL was in the 8th season, between the Delhi Daredevils and the Rajasthan Royals. Who is the only player to have featured in both the matches (and ended up in the losing side on both occasions)?
4. One of these two cricketers playing in the IPL was the first from his country to hit a Test match triple

century. The other was nicknamed 'Mr Cricket'. Both had scored a century on their IPL debut. Name the two cricketers in question.

5. Which leg spinner took a hat-trick in only two legal deliveries in an IPL game?

6. The rivalry between which two IPL teams is known as 'South Indian Derby'?

7. What is the official mascot of Rajasthan Royals known as?

8. What is the tagline for the erstwhile IPL franchise 'Deccan Chargers'?

9. The logo of the Mumbai Indians franchise is a modern rendering of which entity?

10. Which IPL team's mascot is called 'Hoog Lee'?

11. Which IPL franchise has the tagline, 'All the king's men'?

12. Which IPL franchise is owned by IndiaWin Sports?

13. Which notable musician in Kollywood composed the team anthem for Sunrisers Hyderabad?

14. What is said to be the inspiration for the Karnataka Flag? It also serves as the inspiration for the jersey of RCB.

15. Who is the only non-Indian player to get the 'emerging player of the year award' in the IPL?

16. Delhi Daredevils franchise has changed its name. We will see it in the 2019 Indian Premier League. What is

the changed name?

17. Which brand will be the official title sponsor for IPL in the timeframe between 2019-2022?

18. Which multimedia company came up with a fictional IPL team called 'Chonkpur Cheetahs'?

19. Who was the first batsman to be dismissed by hit wicket in the IPL?

20. Who is the first Afghan player to play in the IPL?

21. Who is the first player from Nepal to get an IPL contract?

22. Who is the first Indian to score a century in IPL?

23. Who had designed the IPL Trophy?

24. Who was the first player to be dismissed for a Golden Duck in IPL?

25. Who had bowled the first maiden over in the IPL?

26. Who had taken the first wicket in the IPL?

27. Who was the first cricketer to take a catch in the IPL?

28. Who had won the first Man of the Match award in the IPL?

29. Name the first Indian to win the Orange Cap.

30. This left-arm fast bowler who played for the Rajasthan Royals was known for his pace in the 2009 IPL. Unfortunately, he faded into obscurity after his action was declared 'suspect'. Shane Warne was impressed with him and he went on to play for Pune Warriors India. Who is this bowler?

31. This leg-spinner and all-rounder from Mumbai was spotted at a cricket talent hunt reality show. He was picked by Rajasthan Royals in 2008 and won praise from his captain Shane Warne. Who is this player?

32. This South African left-arm seamer took 12 wickets for Kings XI Punjab in 2009, including two four-wicket hauls. He has also played two T20s for his national team. Who is this player?

33. This wicketkeeper was named the emerging player of the year, in 2008, when he played for Royal Challengers Bangalore. He has also played for Bengal in the Ranji Trophy. Who is this cricketer?

34. Delhi Daredevils entered the 2017 season with the dubious record of having ten captains in the past. Virender Sehwag was the first, while Zaheer Khan is the latest, but who was the first overseas player to captain the Delhi Daredevils?

35. Andrew Leipus, who is the physiotherapist for Kolkata Knight Riders, has a unique 3-digit number on his jersey. This was in reference to a well-known number which one would remember in times of emergency. Which number does Leipus wear?

36. While playing for Royal Challengers in 2009, this person had to see his sister celebrate his dismissal. This was because she was a cheerleader for the Chennai Super Kings, whom they were facing. He said in an interview—*'I don't mind, really. Except, she really*

did seem to be doing her job very well when I was out. She didn't have to look so pleased.' Who is this not-so-happy brother?

37. In the 2013 Indian Premier League, playing in his last ever match, this player (and captain) decided to bowl off-spin to Harbhajan Singh. He proceeded to get a wicket off the only ball he ever bowled in T20 cricket, though he has played more than hundred T20 matches. Who is this player?

38. In 2015 Indian Premier League, the Delhi Daredevils wore lavender coloured jerseys. This was in association with a cricketer's foundation which was raising awareness about cancer. The foundation belonged to which player?

39. Who was the only player to have been in both the first and the 500th (RR vs DD, 2015) IPL matches?

40. He is a former Purple Cap winner and has taken more than 100 wickets in the Indian Premier League. He has also led his side successfully in an ICC World T20 final. Name him.

41. Hashim Amla achieved this unfortunate distinction twice. Rishabh Pant was the last to achieve this distinction while Andrew Symonds was the first to hold this distinction. Others in the list include Virat Kohli and Steve Smith. Which distinction is being talked about?

42. Nanji Kalidas Mehta was behind the foundation of

this conglomerate. The group's businesses include investments in sugar, cement, packaging and insurance. The conglomerate is part-owner of which IPL franchise?

43. He was one of the top five wicket takers in the first IPL. He played two ODIs for India. In 2012, he achieved a rare first in the history of top flight T20 cricket by bowling 3 maidens in a match. Identify him.

44. Whose first three IPL wickets (taken in a single match at the Eden Gardens in May 2008) were Virender Sehwag, Gautam Gambhir and AB de Villiers?

45. Who is the only person to be the coach of an IPL winning, as well as an ICC World Cup winning team?

46. Chirag Suri was bought by the Gujarat Lions in the 2017 Indian Premier League auction. Which team did he represent in international cricket?

47. Shikhar Dhawan was traded to which team prior to the 2019 Indian Premier League auction?

48. A famous personality who has been associated with the Indian Premier League for a decade made this statement recently: *'It is illogical to me to replace me with somebody who is almost my mirror image. That, to me, is the one area that hurts.'* Who is he?

49. Ahead of the first Qualifier match of the 2018 Indian Premier League, the BCCI organized a women's exhibition match. Which two star Indian players were captains of the two teams?

50. Despite being on the losing side, who had the most economical figures (for all bowlers who completed their 4 over spell) in the 2018 Indian Premier League final?

Answers

1. 4
2. Michael Clarke
3. Zaheer Khan
4. Brendon McCullum and Michael Hussey
5. Pravin Tambe for Rajasthan Royals in 2014
6. Chennai Super Kings and Royal Challengers Bangalore
7. Moochu Singh
8. The Unstoppables
9. Sudarshan Chakra
10. Kolkata Knight Riders (named after river Hoogli)
11. Kolkata Knight Riders
12. Mumbai Indians
13. G. V. Prakash Kumar (A.R Rahman's nephew)
14. Turmeric and Kumkum
15. Mustafizur Rahman
16. Delhi Capitals
17. Vivo
18. Amazon
19. Musavir Khote
20. Rashid Khan
21. Sandeep Lamichhane
22. Manish Pandey

23. ORRA Designs headed by Mona Mehta had designed the IPL Trophy
24. Chaminda Vaas
25. Glenn Mcgrath
26. Zaheer Khan took the wicket of Saurav Ganguly which is the first fallen wicket in the IPL
27. Jacques Kallis took the catch of Saurav Ganguly
28. Brendon McCullum
29. Sachin Tendulkar
30. Kamran Khan
31. Dinesh Salunkhe
32. Yusuf Abdullah
33. Shreevats Goswami
34. James Hopes
35. 911
36. Jacques Kallis. His sister Janine, a dancer and physiotherapist was part of CSK's cheerleading squad
37. Adam Gilchrist
38. Yuvraj Singh
39. Zaheer Khan
40. Lasith Malinga
41. Scoring an IPL hundred in a losing cause
42. Kolkata Knight Riders
43. Manpreet Gony

44. Shoaib Akhtar
45. Darren Lehmann
46. United Arab Emirates
47. Delhi Capitals
48. Richard Madley on being replaced by Hugh Edmeades as the auctioneer for the IPL
49. Smriti Mandhana and Harmanpreet Kaur
50. Bhuvneshwar Kumar

EPILOGUE

As we write this, the preparations are on for Season 12—IPL 2019. After initial speculation that the coming season might be shifted abroad due to the General Elections, it was declared that the entirety of the series will be held in India. We are quite sure that it will be bigger and better than the previous seasons. It will take the viewers through a dizzying array of emotions and provide memories that will last for many years. Some of the records that we have discussed in this book might be broken, some new ones might get set and many new names will make their mark. We shall sit and diligently note down everything as we look forward to compiling and writing a follow-up to this book.

ACKNOWLEDGEMENTS

The authors wish to acknowledge the creative input, support and motivation provided by friends and family.

Berty Ashley—To Akhila Phadnis for re-igniting my love for cricket and for the shared memories of CSK and South Africa. To Rishikesh and Rishwin, from Madurai, for their input. To S. Winifred for starting him off on cricket.

Titash Banerjea—To Debduti Banerjee for tolerating the alarm bells ringing at 5 am...just so I could watch a cricket match...to all the members of Enquiry—the Jadavpur University quiz club—my favourite bunch of people in the world. To my uncle Souvik Banerjea for introducing me to quizzing.

Both authors would like to thank Kunal Mundal for bringing them together, and the people of the Cluesday Whatsapp group and MFC for all their love and support (and the hundreds of messages that we have to clear every morning).